LIVING
— WITH —
DIABETES

A JOURNAL FOR TEENS

JAIMIE A. WOLFELT

Companion
P R E S S

An imprint of the Center for Loss and Life Transition | Fort Collins, Colorado

Contents

Introduction

I was diagnosed with Type 1 diabetes three weeks before my tenth birthday. I still have vivid memories of moments during that time. I was terrified and didn't understand what was happening or what living with Type 1 really meant for my life. As I grew through my teenage years and into my twenties, I experienced many—if not all—of the mental, emotional, and social issues discussed in this journal. Now, as a 25-year-old, I still experience some of the challenges that I will outline in the coming chapters.

I kept a diabetes journal from the day I was diagnosed until I went to college. As I reread my journal now, I'm reminded of how much I struggled during my teen years. There were moments where I was extremely angry at diabetes and wished that I could have lived a different life. I questioned why I had diabetes and others didn't; I even questioned the meaning of the world. There were days when I was scared of changing my diabetes management and times where I wanted to give up because it never seemed to go right. I took on a lot of responsibility too fast and ended up blaming myself for having high A1Cs. I made myself feel horrible and dreaded going to the doctor to see how my next A1C would value my personal worth. I felt as though no one understood me or how I felt. For years, I didn't really know anyone else with Type 1. Overall, I was angry at my family and my doctors for telling me how to manage a disease that they would never know how it truly felt to live with.

It wasn't until I found a group of friends with Type 1 that I started to feel understood and less ashamed of my diabetes. I found power in my friends with diabetes and leaned on them for support and inspiration. As I became a young adult, I met more and more people living with diabetes who truly embraced their lives. They weren't afraid to talk about diabetes. They wore their insulin pumps for all to see, while I had been hiding mine for years. I was inspired by their spirit and their embrace of managing diabetes. They taught me to embrace mine. Although we all acknowledged the hardships of living with Type 1, we also honored what we had gained from living with diabetes. I now proudly show my insulin pump and CGM. I get excited when I have the opportunity to teach others about living with Type 1, and I am extremely passionate about diabetes advocacy, education, and connecting with other T1Ds.

I have come to appreciate all of the things that I've learned from living with diabetes. What's more, I've been able to integrate what I've learned into a meaningful part of my identity. I have learned responsibility and maturity, how to appreciate my body and health, how to listen to my body, how to have empathy and compassion for others and for myself, and I have discovered my true passion. I want to help others who live with Type 1.

GLOSSARY OF TERMS USED IN THIS BOOK

A1C
A blood test that measures your average blood sugar level over the past three months

BG
Blood glucose, or blood sugar

CGM
Continuous glucose monitor (e.g., Dexcom, Libre, Medtronic, etc.)

DKA
Diabetic ketoacidosis. A dangerous and serious reaction in your body to low insulin. Ketones can build up and make you feel sick. Can lead to diabetic coma and death.

JDRF
A nonprofit organization that funds Type 1 research and advocacy for people living with Type 1; formerly called the Juvenile Diabetes Research Foundation

Low Treatment
Food you eat to increase your blood sugar when you have a low

T1D
Type 1 diabetes, or a person who lives with Type 1 diabetes

I'm working on my master's degree in counseling, and one day soon I will counsel children, teens, adults, and families living with Type 1 and help them find meaning and embrace life with diabetes. Most of all, I hope to help others going through challenging times with diabetes so they learn to thrive and live healthy and full lives.

WHY I WROTE THIS JOURNAL

Type 1 diabetes is a lifelong journey full of different obstacles. I believe that the teenage and young adult years are some of the most difficult and challenging to live through as a person with Type 1. Virtually all young people struggle during their teen years to understand who they truly are. They are continually challenged by emotional, social, and physical issues. Type 1 diabetes adds another layer to the challenges that all teens face.

To my readers—I hope that this journal helps you learn about and express your emotions and thoughts related to a wide range of issues you may face living with Type 1. My biggest hope is that this book reminds you that you are not alone. You are experiencing challenges that many fellow Type 1 people have experienced before. Know that you can live through these experiences and learn from them. Diabetes is a part of your life, but it is not your entire life. It is only one part of you—a part that you can learn from and integrate into the person you are so you can live a full and happy life.

I encourage you to use this journal as a release for some of the more painful, irritating, ambivalent, or emotional experiences you have living with Type 1. This journal is for you and your story. So if you feel like you're having a tough day and one chapter is calling out to you more than the others, I invite you to skip around and choose the content you need. When I pose questions for your journal responses, feel free to answer all or none of the questions. They are just jumping-off points, and you are free to respond to the content in any way that is meaningful to you. In addition, I encourage you to find ways that are helpful and fun for you to express the emotions and experiences discussed in this book . If you don't feel like writing, you can create a piece of art, draw, paint, sculpt, write a poem or a song, create music, play the keys on the piano that fit with the emotion you are feeling, create a dance, or find a song that fits with your emotions and listen to it with your eyes closed. Expressing your thoughts and feelings is essential to your mental health, but do it in ways that work for you.

Finally, if you're having a hard time with anything discussed in this journal, please reach out to an adult you trust, speak to your doctor, and talk to a counselor. You are not alone.

Thank you for using this journal.

With love,

Jaimie A. Wolfelt

Jaimie A. Wolfelt

CHAPTER ONE:

Your Diagnosis Story

The moment of your Type 1 diagnosis was one of the most pivotal of your life. That day and the days following changed your life forever. Some of you may have memories of your diagnosis, and others may have been too young to remember. But even if you were diagnosed as a small child, I'm sure you've been told the story by your caregivers. This story is significant to your diabetes journey and to your life in general.

Although you've probably shared this story with others many times, it's important that you tell this story to yourself too. When we express our memories, we're creating a story within ourselves. We're creating meaning and are able to process some of the more painful emotions that are experienced with the story. By telling your story, you're creating a piece of you; you may be able to find new insight, gain a new perspective, or understand a part of yourself that was hiding. If you don't discover these things right away, that's OK; they may come later on. In addition, by writing about your diagnosis, you will record a piece of your own history that you can look back on for years to come.

As you tell the story of your diagnosis below, feel free to write about any and all emotions and experiences that come to mind. Write about any memories or stories that stick out to you from that time. You can write about the time leading up to your diagnosis, the day of your diagnosis, and the weeks or months following your diagnosis. Embrace the feelings that come while you are writing. Allow them to be felt and experienced. All emotions belong. Through feeling your emotions and expressing your experiences, you can truly process some of the deeply held anxieties that may be hiding there.

My Type 1 diabetes diagnosis story

_____

_____

_____

_____

_____

_____

_____

_____

_____

_____

_____

_____

_____

_____

_____

_____

What feelings did you experience while you thought back on and wrote about your diagnosis?

_____

_____

_____

_____

_____

_____

_____

_____

_____

_____

_____

_____

I hope that revisiting this time of your life has helped you reconnect with some of the emotions that diabetes has stirred within you. Telling your story is an essential part of living with Type 1 and being able to eventually accept the diagnosis. I don't expect everyone using this journal to have accepted their diagnosis yet or to accept it by the time they finish this journal, but I believe that interacting with this journal can be a steppingstone to getting there. In order to truly live fully, we must accept the grief that comes from being diagnosed with a lifelong chronic illness. Telling your story can help with this.

CHAPTER TWO:

Sadness

It's natural for your diagnosis story to bring up some sadness within you. Chronic illness brings many losses. Along the way, you may have felt loss of health, loss of safety, loss of control, loss of hope, loss of vitality, loss of freedom, and more. You may feel these losses throughout your journey with diabetes, and they may hit you unexpectedly at different times. I know I experienced a lot of loss in the months after my diagnosis. I'd have times where I suddenly felt sorry for myself because I had to deal with diabetes and other kids my age did not. When you are feeling these kinds of losses, you are experiencing grief. To process your grief and allow for growth through your losses, you must express these losses and the feelings of sadness that come with them. To move through intense emotions is to experience and express them.

For this journal entry, I want to encourage you to allow yourself to experience any sadness that comes with living with Type 1. It's OK to have sorrow for our own situations. Allow yourself to feel sorry for yourself and experience your sadness.

What makes you sad about living with Type 1 diabetes?

_____

_____

_____

_____

_____

_____

_____

_____

_____

_____

What types of losses associated with your diabetes have made you feel sad, both for yourself and for others?

_____

_____

_____

_____

_____

_____

_____

_____

_____

Feeling sad is a natural part of life and loss. You have experienced losses in your life due to Type 1. It's healthy for you to allow yourself to experience the sadness that comes with these losses and express it. When you're feeling sad about diabetes, I encourage you to activate that sadness and move through it by expressing it. You can take a walk, exercise, meditate, create a piece of art or music, dance, listen to a song, talk with a friend or loved one, or do anything that will move your heart and soul.

What is one way you can express your sadness the next time you feel it?

_____

_____

_____

_____

_____

_____

_____

_____

_____

_____

_____

_____

I also want to encourage you to have compassion for yourself. When you're feeling down, try to talk to yourself like you would talk to a best friend—showing true compassion and care for your situation.

How can you show compassion for yourself?

_____

_____

_____

_____

_____

_____

_____

_____

_____

_____

_____

_____

_____

_____

_____

_____

_____

Remember that you are a human being, and all human beings have tough times. Be kind to yourself.

CHAPTER THREE:

Anger

Another natural reaction to loss is feelings of anger. Living with Type 1 diabetes can create a lot of anger. As a teen, I felt angry at diabetes, angry at my body, angry that I had diabetes and others didn't, angry at my doctors, angry at my parents, and generally angry at the world. To this day, although I have processed a lot of this anger, I still experience it when my blood sugar is low at an inconvenient time, when a high blood sugar won't go down, or when I've tried extremely hard to get my numbers in range and nothing seems to be working.

In order to process anger, you must express it. Intense emotions call for expression in order to be released from your body and mind.

For this journal entry, allow yourself to reflect on times you've been angry about living with diabetes. Accept these feelings. The world may make you feel like anger is not an acceptable emotion to show, but anger is a natural part of life that demands to be felt and expressed.

What makes you angry about living with Type 1 diabetes?

_____

_____

_____

_____

_____

_____

_____

_____

_____

_____

_____

_____

_____

_____

_____

_____

_____

_____

_____

_____

I hope that you experienced some relief when reflecting on your anger. When we don't express our anger, it can eat us up from the inside out. It can consume us with fury and make us mad at the world.

In what circumstances do you find yourself getting angry about living with Type 1, and how does that anger feel in your body?

_____

_____

_____

_____

_____

_____

_____

_____

_____

_____

_____

_____

_____

The next time you get mad about diabetes, allow the anger to come. Have compassion for yourself. Again, it's natural for you to have anger, and you are allowed to feel it.

I encourage you to find ways to express anger through your body. For example, you can punch your bed, scream into a pillow, go on a run, or rip up some paper. Whatever works for you to safely release some of that angry energy that builds up in your body—do that.

What are some ways you would like to try expressing your anger in the future?

CHAPTER FOUR

Fluctuating Blood Sugar

Another factor that can affect your mood is fluctuating blood sugar levels. For a person living with diabetes, the teenage years are usually some of the most challenging for fluctuating blood sugar due to puberty and hormonal changes. So, if you're experiencing this, it's completely normal—and also extremely frustrating. When your blood sugar is going up and down throughout the day, it can have rollercoaster effects on your body and emotions. I tend to feel angry when my blood sugar is high or ramping up really fast, and when my blood sugar is low, I feel annoyed. When I have a day of up and down blood sugars, I feel frustrated and tired, and I usually blame myself for what's happened with my blood sugar. This can create a lot of negative emotions and be a recipe for a negative self-image.

what emotions do you feel when your blood sugar is high?

_____

_____

_____

_____

_____

_____

How about when your BGs are low?

How do you feel when you've had a day where your blood sugars seem to go up and down all day?

_____

_____

_____

_____

_____

_____

_____

_____

_____

_____

_____

_____

_____

When you have emotional reactions to blood sugar levels, I want to remind you again to be kind to yourself. There are so many factors that affect blood sugar levels, and humans are not pancreases. We can't perfectly predict how our body will be affected. In addition, remember that your blood sugar is not a representation of you or your personal worth; it is a piece of information. You can use this information to make your next decision as well as store away the information for background on what to do next time. You are worth more than your blood sugars.

Write a little more about your issues with and feelings about blood sugar levels.

_____

_____

_____

_____

_____

_____

_____

_____

_____

_____

_____

_____

_____

_____

_____

_____

_____

Anxiety

Teens and young adults living with Type 1 diabetes are at a significantly higher risk for developing anxiety than their non-diabetic peers. Make a checkmark next to any anxiety symptoms you've experienced.

Symptoms of anxiety:

- Feeling nervous, restless, or tense
- A sense of impending danger, panic, or doom
- Increased heart rate
- Rapid breathing
- Sweating
- Trembling
- Feeling weak or tired
- Trouble concentrating or thinking about anything other than the present worry
- Trouble sleeping
- Gastrointestinal problems

Do you experience any of these symptoms? If so, which ones and under what circumstances?

_____

_____

_____

_____

_____

_____

_____

_____

_____

_____

_____

_____

Living with Type 1 as a young person can create anxiety in many ways. Some factors that researchers have found can increase anxiety for Type 1 teens are:

- Managing diabetes stress added to overall daily stress
- Fear of low blood sugar
- Increased anxiety due to low family support
- Fear of negative judgment by others

You have a lot more to think about and worry about throughout the day than most of your peers. Some of the things that you do every day can affect your body, mind, and overall life and well-being, while most teens don't have to worry about these kinds of issues.

If you do experience anxiety, what makes you feel anxious? What about living with diabetes makes you feel anxious?

How do you feel knowing that you have a higher risk for anxiety because you live with T1D?

_____

_____

_____

_____

_____

_____

_____

_____

_____

_____

_____

_____

_____

_____

_____

I hope you know that you are not alone. Many people living with Type 1 diabetes experience anxiety. I myself have experienced a lot of anxiety through my journey with diabetes. In fact, I still do. I physically feel anxiety as a weight on my chest.

If you experience anxiety, where do you feel it in your body?

_____

_____

_____

_____

_____

_____

_____

_____

_____

_____

_____

_____

There are many ways you can help yourself when you're feeling anxious. The first method is to remember to breathe, take deep breaths, and focus only on your breathing. Try to quiet your mind and only think of your breath. Breathe in through your nose for four counts and out through your mouth for four counts. Continue to do this for at least five breaths in and out. I would also recommend meditation. Anyone can meditate; you just have to learn and practice. You can find YouTube videos that guide you through easy beginner meditations.

What ways have helped you manage your anxiety in the past? What new methods do you want to try in the future?

_____

_____

_____

_____

_____

_____

_____

_____

_____

_____

_____

_____

_____

Finally, if your anxiety is interfering with your life, I urge you to get some extra help. If you checked off three or more of the symptoms of anxiety at the start of this chapter, experience an overwhelming amount of anxiety, or have had anxiety affect your ability to function, please reach out to a trusted adult, your doctor, or a counselor for help.

CHAPTER SIX:

Depression

People of all ages with Type 1 diabetes are at twice the risk for depression compared to those without diabetes. In addition, researchers have found that teens with Type 1 experience more severe symptoms, a longer duration of symptoms, and a higher rate of recurrence of depression.

Symptoms of depression:

- Feelings of sadness, tearfulness, emptiness, or hopelessness
- Angry outbursts, irritability, or frustration, even over small matters
- Loss of interest or pleasure in most or all normal activities
- Sleep disturbances, including insomnia or sleeping too much
- Tiredness and lack of energy
- Reduced appetite and weight loss or increased cravings for food and weight gain
- Anxiety, agitation, or restlessness
- Slowed thinking, speaking, or body movements
- Feelings of worthlessness or guilt, fixating on past failures or self-blame
- Trouble thinking, concentrating, making decisions, and remembering things
- Frequent or recurrent thoughts of death, suicidal thoughts, suicide attempts
- Unexplained physical problems

These symptoms do not have to relate directly to having Type 1. Depression can be a secondary effect from the challenges of living with Type 1.

Do you experience any of these symptoms? If so, which ones? when do you feel them?

Do you ever feel depressed about living with diabetes? If so, how?

_____

_____

_____

_____

_____

_____

_____

_____

_____

_____

_____

_____

_____

_____

_____

_____

_____

_____

_____

_____

_____

What do you do when you feel depressed?

_____

_____

_____

_____

_____

_____

_____

_____

_____

_____

_____

_____

I want to emphasize that although depression can make you feel extremely alone, you are not alone. Many T1Ds of all ages have experienced depression or live with depression. I myself was diagnosed with depression as a young adult. I still have times in my life where I struggle with depression, but I have also found ways to live and thrive while living with depression. Depression is something that cannot be treated in darkness. It makes you want to live in darkness and convinces you that no one can help, but this is not true. The truth is that in order to live a healthy and full life, you must have others help you when you are feeling depressed.

Please write about your feelings about your higher risk for depression. Also share your thoughts about the fact that you are not alone and that you need others when you are depressed.

_____

_____

_____

_____

_____

_____

_____

_____

_____

_____

_____

_____

_____

_____

_____

_____

_____

_____

If you have continuing depression, the best treatment is to seek help from others and to see a therapist. I urge you to reach out to your caregivers and tell them what is going on. Find a trusted adult who will listen to you and help you get the help you need.

And if you ever experience suicidal thoughts, please tell a trusted adult immediately. You must seek help and not be ashamed for needing it. Everyone in this world needs help in different ways. It makes you strong and responsible to be able to admit when you need help and get it. If you ever begin to make suicide plans, immediately call the National Suicide Prevention Lifeline at 1-800-273-8255 or 911.

CHAPTER SEVEN:

Diabetes Fatigue

There is a specific type of fatigue experienced by people living with diabetes. Fatigue is defined as persistent tiredness and experiencing times when rest does not alleviate feelings of tiredness. It is common for people living with diabetes to experience chronic fatigue due to the effects of living with diabetes. Some factors that contribute to fatigue are fluctuating blood sugar levels, loss of sleep, and 24/7 management.

I'm sure many of you have experienced loss of sleep due to diabetes. In the middle of the night you might be woken up by an alarm—alerting you that your blood sugar is out of range, your insulin pump battery is low, or your insulin cartridge is running out of insulin. Or maybe you wake up because a caregiver comes to check on you. Or maybe you have to pee because your blood sugar is high. There are so many different ways that diabetes disrupts our sleep, because even when we are sleeping, we have to manage our diabetes. Even waking up just to press some buttons on your pump can disrupt your sleep and make your sleep quality decrease significantly.

It's exhausting to live with Type 1 diabetes. You never get a break, and the relentlessness of the demands can take a toll on your mind and body.

Do you experience chronic fatigue? How does your diabetes contribute to your tiredness?

what emotions do you experience about being tired a lot?

_____

_____

_____

_____

_____

_____

_____

_____

_____

_____

_____

_____

_____

_____

By identifying the ways in which diabetes contributes to our tiredness, we can give ourselves more compassion for living with fatigue. I know that I can become frustrated with my tiredness. It makes me sad sometimes that I don't have more energy. I have to constantly remind myself to take care of my body and have compassion for myself; most of the time it's not my fault that I'm tired or feeling unmotivated.

How do you manage your tiredness?

_____

_____

_____

_____

_____

_____

_____

_____

_____

_____

_____

_____

_____

Sometimes the best thing to do is listen to our bodies and rest when we need it. Some other ways that help chronic fatigue is to exercise regularly, eat healthfully, get seven to nine hours of uninterrupted sleep each night if possible, manage and limit stress, and seek support from others.

what are some ways you want to start managing chronic fatigue?

_____

_____

_____

_____

_____

_____

_____

_____

_____

_____

_____

_____

_____

_____

_____

_____

_____

Notes

CHAPTER EIGHT:

Diabetic Burnout

Another unique experience that is specific to people who live with diabetes is "diabetic burnout." This is when a person with diabetes gets frustrated and overwhelmed by the many challenges and responsibilities that come with living with diabetes and they begin to pay less attention to their diabetes management. It's very common for teens to experience this, but it can happen at any age. When this occurs, the person usually doesn't monitor their blood sugar or take insulin as often as they should. It can also be seen in other ways, such as not wanting to receive help from others, being annoyed with alarms from pumps or CGMs, or getting frustrated with caregivers when they ask about diabetes. Some experience mild symptoms and may just feel overwhelmed by diabetes, and others may have more dangerous symptoms. It can result in a high A1C and may contribute to feelings of sadness, anxiety, and depression or vice versa. Diabetic burnout can be extremely harmful and dangerous. In extreme cases, it can lead to diabetic ketoacidosis (DKA), hospitalization, or even death.

Have you had any experiences of burnout? If so, what was it like?

_____

_____

_____

_____

_____

_____

_____

_____

_____

_____

_____

_____

Don't be ashamed if you have experienced any degree of burnout. For people who have lived many years with Type 1 and are tired of the daily management that is required to stay healthy, it's common and understandable. For teens, it's common because it may be the first time you've taken on the full responsibility of living with Type 1. It can be exhausting to realize the full weight of that responsibility.

what thoughts or emotions have you had when you've felt burned out?

_____

_____

_____

_____

_____

_____

_____

_____

_____

_____

_____

_____

_____

_____

_____

_____

_____

I urge you again to have self-compassion. Any emotions you experience are accepted and allowed. Most of your peers who do not live with Type 1 don't have as much responsibility for their health and well-being as you do. So it's natural to feel burned out at times.

If you have ever been in DKA or have burned out and not taken as much insulin as your body needs: How did your body feel when it was not receiving enough insulin?

_____

_____

_____

_____

_____

_____

_____

_____

_____

_____

_____

_____

_____

_____

It's important to remember how your body feels when it doesn't get as much insulin as it needs. Whenever you have this feeling, it's a cue that your body is in an unhealthy state. However, when you consistently have high blood sugar and don't take enough insulin for your blood sugar to be in a healthy range, you can start to get used to your body feeling bad. In other words, poor health starts to feel normal. This is a risk of diabetic burnout. If you sustain it for too long, you get used to how your body feels at a consistently high blood sugar and you forget how it feels to feel healthy. When you are experiencing high blood sugar, you may experience symptoms such as fatigue, increased thirst, and frequent urination.

If you have experienced this, it is when your A1C stays consistently above 8.5 or so and you feel "low" when you are in a healthy range, such as around 100 mg/dL. Although you may feel normal when your blood sugar is high, a T1D who is consistently in range will feel the symptoms of a high blood sugar if it sustains for a couple of hours. Acclimating to high blood sugar in this way is dangerous. If it happens to you, please consult your doctor right away to reevaluate your dosing so that you are receiving the right amount of insulin. If you aren't receiving the right amount of insulin due to burnout and not taking as much on purpose, then you need to seek out help from your doctor or a counselor.

I have had times where I experienced diabetic burnout, and I have had many friends who've experienced it as well. It's extremely frustrating to live with Type 1. When you get to a place of burnout, it can feel like there is no hope. You feel like even if you take care of yourself, it won't matter because you have a chronic illness. I understand these feelings, and I have had them before.

However, there is hope. Diabetes is rough, but it's not impossible. There is a reason to take care of yourself. You are important, and you have an important life to live. Please take care of yourself now and always. How you take care of your diabetes now will determine your health for the rest of your life. I know there are days when you want to give up, and that's OK. Let one of your guardians do all of your diabetes care that day. Tell them today you need a break. Tomorrow you can do it again. Give yourself breaks, but remember that you are strong and that your health and your body create your future.

Write about your feelings about taking good care of yourself and getting help when you need it.

_____

_____

_____

_____

_____

_____

_____

_____

_____

_____

_____

_____

_____

_____

_____

If you are wrestling with burnout or feel as though there is no point in taking care of yourself, please tell someone you trust, contact your doctor, and speak to a counselor.

CHAPTER NINE:

Living with Complications

As I'm sure most of you know, Type 1 diabetes comes with a long list of potential complications later in life if your diabetes is not managed well. Even though they may seem far in the future, it can be terrifying and anxiety-provoking to think about these complications. As a kid, I made myself avoid thinking about them because they gave me so much anxiety. For this chapter, I would like us to be able to think about them and reflect on how they make us feel. The most important thing to remember is that if you take care of your diabetes now and in the future, you have a much lower likelihood of experiencing these complications.

Potential complications of unmanaged Type 1 diabetes:

• Heart and blood vessel disease

• Nerve damage

• Kidney damage

• Eye damage

• Foot damage

• Skin and mouth conditions

• Pregnancy complications

Allow yourself to experience and feel any emotions that come after looking at this list.

How do you feel?

_____

_____

_____

_____

_____

_____

_____

_____

_____

_____

_____

_____

_____

_____

_____

_____

_____

_____

_____

_____

what scares you the most about this list?

_____

_____

_____

_____

_____

_____

_____

_____

_____

_____

_____

_____

_____

_____

_____

It's OK to be scared by this list. No one wants to think about a future in which their health could be in extreme danger or their future could be negatively impacted by their health. It's challenging to accept the responsibility that comes with diabetes and managing your health in order to try to avoid these complications. It's a very heavy load to carry.

How does it feel to have this responsibility? Allow yourself to experience any and all emotions that come with this.

_____

_____

_____

_____

_____

_____

_____

_____

_____

_____

_____

_____

_____

_____

_____

_____

_____

Remember that for now you still have access to help from many caregivers; lean on them for support and to lessen the responsibility sometimes. You will always have people you can go to for support in the future as well: your partner, your friends, your T1D friends, your doctor, a counselor, and more. You are not alone. You are surrounded by people who can help you with your diabetes, and you can find more people to support you if needed. Your friends with T1D will know exactly how you feel and will always be willing to listen to you and be there for you when you are feeling overwhelmed.

who can you go to for support?

_____

_____

_____

_____

_____

_____

_____

_____

_____

_____

_____

_____

_____

_____

Speak to your endocrinologist if you have any questions or concerns about the complications of unmanaged Type 1 diabetes.

Notes

CHAPTER TEN

Balancing Diabetes

One of the most important ways to manage life with diabetes is through balance. We all have to find ways to balance our time and energy among our social, educational, work, family, self-care, and personal worlds. For us, living with diabetes is another part of our world that we have to balance and learn to incorporate into every aspect of our lives. With everything else we have going on, this can be extremely challenging.

How do you manage diabetes while also balancing all of the other aspects of your life?

_____

_____

_____

_____

_____

_____

_____

_____

What makes it hard to manage diabetes and balance everything else in your life?

_____

_____

_____

_____

_____

_____

_____

_____

_____

_____

_____

_____

_____

_____

Actually, managing diabetes is a balancing act all its own. We have to balance insulin, food, exercise, sleep, stress, and more in order to keep ourselves healthy. It's a lot of responsibility to manage all of these things at once.

How good do you feel you are at balancing your diabetes management?

What are some ways you'd like to get better at balancing your diabetes management?

_____

_____

_____

_____

_____

_____

_____

_____

_____

_____

_____

_____

_____

_____

_____

_____

_____

It's OK if you haven't found a way to balance everything and make your life just how you would like it to be. As you grow older, you'll continually learn more about creating a life that makes you happy and is healthy for your body.

In an ideal world, how do you imagine your balanced future?

_____

_____

_____

_____

_____

_____

_____

_____

_____

_____

_____

_____

_____

_____

_____

_____

_____

_____

_____

_____

_____

What emotions come up for you when you think about balance and diabetes?

_____

_____

_____

_____

_____

_____

_____

_____

_____

_____

_____

_____

Remember again to have compassion for yourself. It takes growth and experience to find balance, and there will be times in your life where you will feel unbalanced. Let these times be lessons for the balanced future you imagine. Let yourself live in the unbalanced state and accept it for what it is. Seek out others for help when you want more balance in your life. Your doctors, caregivers, friends, fellow T1Ds, counselors, nutritionists, trainers, and coaches are there to support you and help you balance your world.

CHAPTER ELEVEN:

Body Image

A positive body image is extremely important to creating a strong sense of self-esteem and confidence. If you don't have a very positive body image, you are more likely to feel sad, anxious, depressed, angry, and embarrassed. This applies to all people of all sexes and genders.

Of course, as you know, living with Type 1 diabetes not only affects your body on the inside, it can also show on the outside. It can create scarring, puffiness, redness, bruising, fluctuation in weight, and more. In addition, having devices attached to your body can also make you feel uncomfortable or self-conscious. You may feel embarrassed about your scars or bruises, and you may try to hide your pump sites, pump, or CGM. I hope that you can access these feelings and allow yourself to express them here.

How do you feel about your body? Reflect on your self-image and confidence.

_____

_____

_____

_____

_____

_____

_____

_____

_____

_____

_____

_____

_____

_____

_____

_____

_____

_____

_____

_____

_____

_____

_____

Teenage years are tough for all people to feel confident in their bodies, but diabetes can add an extra layer of insecurities for some.

How do you feel about your scars or signs of diabetes that are on your body? How do you feel about others seeing these things?

It's OK to be self-conscious about your body. Most teenagers are self-conscious about their bodies. Although diabetes may scar your body or make it different from someone without diabetes, remember that these scars are a sign of how you take care of your body and live a healthy life. Still, it can be hard to accept them, and you may always struggle to accept them.

write about this.

_____

_____

_____

_____

_____

_____

_____

_____

_____

_____

_____

_____

_____

Your body image will be a continually changing aspect in your life. I recommend talking to other people with diabetes about how you feel. They have probably experienced the same things. Talking about and expressing how we feel can lead to release and maybe eventually acceptance. My Type 1 friends helped me learn to be proud of wearing my pump and CGM.

If you are having a hard time with your body image or your weight, I hope you will talk to your caregiver, your doctor, or a counselor.

CHAPTER TWELVE:

Isolation

I believe that one of the hardest things about living with Type 1 is the feeling of isolation. At the beginning of my diabetes journey, I felt extremely alone. Many of us with Type 1 have limited interactions with other T1Ds or don't know any at all when we are first diagnosed. Some of us may know someone who lives with Type 1 but not anyone in our age group. When I was first diagnosed and didn't know anyone, I remember being so angry that the people who were telling me what to do and poking me with needles would never know what it felt like to live like me. I felt so alone with my experience of diabetes.

Do you ever feel alone or isolated? What experiences have you had of feeling isolated with your diabetes?

_____

_____

_____

_____

_____

_____

_____

_____

_____

_____

_____

_____

_____

_____

How did it feel to express your feelings of isolation and aloneness?

_____

_____

_____

_____

_____

_____

_____

_____

_____

_____

I hope by expressing some of these emotions you can feel some release of them. It is normal to feel isolated in your experience of diabetes. Many of us do not have family members with Type 1 and can feel as though no one understands. Allow yourself to feel the sadness that comes with isolation, but also remember that you can find a community!

It wasn't until I had a group of friends with Type 1 diabetes that I felt more understood and less isolated. I met my first group of friends at an American Diabetes Association summer camp! It was so powerful to have friends who had diabetes. They inspired me, and we all felt that we could support and love each other when we were struggling with diabetes. Today, I have so many friends with Type 1 I know I could reach out to for support at any time. They are a huge part of the reason why I thrive while living with diabetes.

Do you have T1D friends? If so, how do they make you feel less isolated?

_____

_____

_____

_____

_____

_____

_____

_____

_____

_____

_____

_____

_____

_____

_____

_____

_____

_____

_____

_____

_____

_____

_____

If you don't have any friends or acquaintances with T1D, you are not alone! I encourage you to find your diabetes community. Check out the American Diabetes Association, Beyond Type 1, and JDRF websites, and look for events you can attend near you!

CHAPTER THIRTEEN:

The Invisibility of Diabetes

Another tricky aspect about living with diabetes is that it's largely an invisible disease. Most of the time, people can't tell that we live with a chronic illness just by looking at us. Although this allows us to live a comfortable life and we don't get too many questions from complete strangers (unless they notice our pump/CGM or when we inject insulin or test BG), it can also create some issues. Since it's not noticeable by outward appearances, people can make rash judgments about us or may not take our needs seriously. This is why it's extremely important to educate others and to advocate for ourselves (both of these subjects will be addressed in later chapters). Still, it's difficult because in some ways we benefit from having an invisible illness, while in other ways it can be extremely frustrating.

What experiences have you had related to living with an invisible illness?

_____

_____

_____

_____

_____

_____

_____

_____

_____

_____

_____

Allow yourself to express all the emotions that come with living with an invisible illness. There are good and bad things that come from it.

How do you feel about it?

_____

_____

_____

_____

_____

_____

_____

_____

_____

Sometimes you may use the invisibility of diabetes to your advantage, and that's OK. We don't always want everyone to know about our diabetes or to have to talk about it all the time. You can allow the invisibility of it to be something you can use in those times.

When do you use the invisibility of diabetes to your advantage? How does it make you feel?

_____

_____

_____

_____

_____

_____

_____

_____

_____

_____

_____

_____

_____

_____

_____

_____

Other times it can be extremely frustrating that people don't understand the hardships of living with Type 1 because it seems invisible to them.

when has it been hard for you to live with a relatively invisible illness? How does it make you feel?

_____

_____

_____

_____

_____

_____

_____

_____

_____

_____

_____

_____

_____

Again, I want you to have self-compassion when you are in either of these situations. It's OK to both appreciate the invisibility and also be frustrated by it. Allow yourself to feel any emotions that arise when you encounter these situations. Find healthy ways to release and express these emotions.

CHAPTER FOURTEEN:

Co-managing Diabetes
with Your Parents/Caregivers

Another challenge of living with diabetes as a teenager is figuring out how to manage diabetes with parents or caregivers. Many of you are probably at different levels of figuring out how to manage your diabetes on your own. As you grow older, you are gradually taking on more responsibility for your diabetes management. Some of you may only be at the beginning of this process, and some of you may be pretty self-sufficient at this point. Either way, if you are still living with your parents or caregivers, you are probably still talking to them about diabetes management. It can be complicated to feel independent yet still have a parent or guardian asking you about how you are taking care of yourself.

How do you split up diabetes management responsibilities with your parents/caregivers?

_____

_____

_____

_____

_____

_____

_____

_____

_____

_____

_____

_____

It's natural for there to be conflict between you and your parents/caregivers when it comes to managing your diabetes.

When do you get upset/frustrated with trying to co-manage diabetes with your parents/caregivers?

_____

_____

_____

_____

_____

_____

_____

_____

_____

_____

_____

_____

_____

_____

How do you feel when your parents/caregivers ask you about your diabetes management?

_____

_____

_____

_____

_____

_____

_____

_____

_____

Although it can be frustrating to co-manage diabetes with your parents/caregivers, they are trying to help because they love you. Sometimes their love is expressed in ways that feel controlling or overbearing, but at the end of the day they love you and want the best for you.

what is one way you are thankful for your parents'/caregivers' help with managing diabetes?

_____

_____

_____

_____

_____

_____

_____

_____

_____

_____

_____

_____

_____

_____

_____

_____

I encourage you to share your gratitude with your parents/caregivers.

What is one thing that you wish your parents/caregivers could do differently to help you with managing diabetes?

_____

_____

_____

_____

_____

_____

_____

_____

_____

_____

_____

_____

_____

_____

_____

_____

If you are having trouble co-managing aspects of your diabetes with your parents or guardians, I encourage you to talk with them. A clear conversation about how you are feeling can communicate your needs and let them know how you would like them to help you with your diabetes management. One way you can prepare for this conservation is by writing out or thinking about the following and using "I statements" when talking to your parent/caregiver.

- Ways that I want to manage my diabetes independently:
  Example: *I would like to be in charge of testing my blood sugar and giving myself insulin.*

- Ways that I want help managing my diabetes:
  Example: *I would like help making sure I always have insulin and diabetes supplies.*

- Ways I can communicate with my parents/guardians about my diabetes:
  Example: *I would like to be in charge of telling my parents/guardians about my numbers every day instead of being asked about it.*

Here is some space for you to brainstorm some of these ideas. Using "I statements" allows for you to take responsibility for your actions without placing blame on your parents/caregivers.

Ways I want to manage my diabetes independently:

_____

_____

_____

_____

_____

_____

_____

_____

_____

_____

_____

_____

_____

_____

_____

_____

Ways that I want help managing my diabetes:

_____

_____

_____

_____

_____

_____

_____

_____

_____

_____

_____

Ways that I can communicate with my parents/guardians about my diabetes:

_____

_____

_____

_____

_____

_____

_____

_____

_____

_____

_____

_____

_____

_____

You can use this as a jumping-off point for a conversation about how you can have a healthy and cooperative relationship with your parents/caregivers around managing diabetes. This is just a starting point, and you will have to compromise with your caregivers to find what works best for everyone.

CHAPTER FIFTEEN:

Stigmas

When someone lives with Type 1 diabetes, they also live with the stigmas that come with it. A stigma is a sense of shame society tends to place on something, even if that something is not inherently bad or anyone's fault. There are many stigmas about both Type 1 and Type 2 that are false and can be hurtful for those who live with them. It can be painful to hear the myths, assumptions, clichés, and jokes. It can be extremely frustrating to see or hear ignorant comments about diabetes on social media, TV, and movies. And when a stranger says something about you that is rooted in stigma and lack of education, it can be extremely hard not to be upset. Most of these things come from a lack of education on diabetes in the general public. Usually the people who repeat or joke about diabetes misconceptions have no understanding about what diabetes is or the differences between Type 1 and Type 2.

Here are just a few of the most common misconceptions I have heard and seen:

• You must be overweight to have diabetes.
• You "got" diabetes by eating too much sugar.
• If you have diabetes, you aren't allowed to eat sugar or any sweets.
• There's a "bad" and a "good" type of diabetes.

For the following journal entries, allow yourself to release and express some of the emotions that you feel when you are upset by diabetes stigmas or misconceptions.

What experiences have you had with stigmas around diabetes? When have you felt hurt or upset by something that was said about diabetes?

How did you feel after you were associated with a stigma?

I know from personal experience that it can be infuriating to stand in front of someone who has made a comment about your life and your body that they do not understand. However, I encourage you to remember that most people are not trying to make you feel bad and are doing the best they can to connect with you and understand your situation. If you feel up to the task, I encourage you to educate the people who make these statements. If you don't, you can refer them to resources such as the American Diabetes Association or the Mayo Clinic. There are many links you can share with others on the differences between Type 1 and Type 2, for example. There are also a lot of YouTube videos explaining stigmas and assumptions about diabetes to those who don't understand. Another way you can address these comments is to be honest with the person who has said them and tell them how their statements are not true and have made you feel. If you are honest in an open and accepting way about how they have hurt you, they will better understand why what they said is inappropriate. When someone hurts you through their assumptions, try to regard them with empathy for their misunderstanding and tell them what your experience with diabetes is like. In addition, try to release any uneasy emotions after you have had this encounter. Talk to a friend, write about it, create a piece of art, exercise, or listen to music. The more anger or uncomfortable feelings you hold within your body, the worse you will feel and the more upset you'll be the next time someone says something inappropriate.

How would you like to release some of the negative emotions the next time you encounter a stigma about diabetes?

_____

_____

_____

_____

_____

Notes:

CHAPTER SIXTEEN:
Advocating for Yourself

In order to live a full and healthy life with Type 1 diabetes, you must advocate for your needs. There may be times in school, sports, work, relationships, social outings, and more where you will have to voice your needs to others. Since there is a lack of understanding in the general population about Type 1 diabetes, there will be times when you have to tell others exactly what you need because they may not understand. If you are having a low blood sugar and don't have a low treatment with you, for example, you will have to have others help you, and you will have to communicate the urgency of the situation. Many do not understand why someone would need juice or candy as fast as possible, and it can be extremely hard to communicate when your blood sugar is low. In addition, you may have times where your blood sugar is going high and you don't have insulin with you or your pump site has come out. You will have to explain to others that you need to go home urgently. There are also times in sports or at work or school where you may need extra accommodations in order for you to stay safe and healthy. It is extremely important that you voice your needs and the urgency of your needs. For some people, voicing their needs may come easily, and for others it can be extremely distressing.

How comfortable are you about voicing your needs to others?

How do you feel about voicing your needs in an urgent situation?

_____

_____

_____

_____

_____

_____

_____

_____

_____

_____

_____

_____

_____

_____

_____

Urgent T1D needs can cause anxiety and a state of panic, especially if your needs are not met. This is why it is so important to be able to advocate for yourself when necessary.

Have you ever had an experience where your needs weren't being met? If so, what happened, and how did it make you feel?

Your needs matter—not just because you have a chronic condition, but because you are a person of value. If you're not comfortable voicing your needs to others, remember that you have value and that your health depends on your ability to be able to communicate your needs. To prepare for these times, make sure you always plan ahead. Have a conversation with your coaches, coworkers and bosses, and teachers proactively, well before any emergency happens. Explain to them what could happen, what the symptoms might look like, and what treatment you might need. If you're going out somewhere, make sure that at least one person you are with is educated about diabetes and can help you get what you need. You can practice communicating your needs ahead of time too. Try role playing these conversations with a parent or close friend.

How would you communicate your needs to others in an urgent situation?

_____

_____

_____

_____

_____

_____

_____

_____

_____

_____

_____

Notes

CHAPTER SEVENTEEN

Sex and Relationships

Every aspect of our lives is affected by living with Type 1, including sex and relationships. The most important thing to do when you are in a committed long-term relationship and/or a sexual relationship is to educate your partner about T1D. You want to make sure they understand what Type 1 is and the urgency of emergency situations. They should know what you need if your BG is low versus when it is high. They should also know what to do if you ever have an urgent low. This is important so that your needs are met and that they can help you when you need it. Even if you are not in a relationship right now, this is something you will want to prepare for and be aware of.

What concerns do you have about being in a relationship and managing your diabetes?

_____

_____

_____

_____

_____

_____

_____

How would you communicate to your partner about your needs?

_____

_____

_____

_____

_____

_____

_____

_____

_____

_____

_____

_____

Sex is also something that is affected by diabetes. Men with Type 1 have a higher risk of developing erectile dysfunction (ED) due to a higher risk of nerve damage. This is another reason why it's important to manage your diabetes now, and in the future, to try to lower your risk of complications. Women with Type 1 have a higher risk of sexual problems (such as low sex drive, and problems with orgasm, etc.) due to higher risk of nerve damage as well as depression, which can also cause these effects.

How do you feel about the effects diabetes can have on sex?
Allow yourself to reflect on any reactions you have.

_____

_____

_____

_____

_____

_____

_____

_____

_____

_____

_____

_____

_____

_____

In addition, if you are having a sexual relationship, you need to make sure that you are being safe. Have a birth control plan and speak to a doctor. In addition, if you're a woman with Type 1, make sure you research and adjust insulin needs accordingly if you take birth control that contains hormones. Most hormones will affect your blood sugar in some way, so talk to your endocrinologist about birth control and managing diabetes.

what is your plan for safe sex and managing diabetes with birth control? How do you feel about this?

_____

_____

_____

_____

_____

_____

_____

_____

_____

_____

_____

_____

Sex is a big responsibility for all young people, and for T1Ds it creates even more. Make sure you have a plan and communicate with your partner about diabetes and your needs. Always make sure you test your blood sugar before sex and have low treatment available if needed. Speak to your doctors about diabetes, sex, and birth control needs. If your parent or caregiver usually accompanies you to doctor visits and you would like to discuss your sexual health privately, you can always ask them to give you some alone time with the doctor each visit.

Notes:

_____

_____

_____

_____

_____

_____

_____

_____

_____

_____

_____

_____

_____

_____

_____

_____

_____

_____

_____

_____

_____

CHAPTER EIGHTEEN

Friends and Diabetes

I'm sure most of your close friends probably don't have Type 1. It can be challenging when the people you spend the most time with don't understand what it's like to live with diabetes. When I was a teen, I remember feeling different because my best friends didn't have the same kinds of responsibilities I did. When we hung out, I would sometimes absentmindedly forget to test my blood sugar or take my insulin for meals or snacks. It bothered me that they could eat food and sugar freely without thought while I had so much more to think about and do.

For this journal chapter, write about any experiences in which you have struggled with spending time with friends who don't have diabetes.

What kinds of things bother you about being different from your friends because you have diabetes?

_____

_____

_____

_____

_____

_____

_____

_____

_____

_____

_____

_____

_____

_____

_____

_____

_____

What emotions do you feel when it seems your friends can't understand things about living with Type 1 diabetes?

_____

_____

_____

_____

_____

There are many things that can be exasperating about having friends who don't have diabetes. I remember times when I found it almost impossible to explain diabetes and the ways it made me feel. I have heard stories about teenagers who try to hide their diabetes from their peers and friends. While I know that some aspects of living with Type 1 can be embarrassing, it's also dangerous to not be honest with people around you. I think the best way to alleviate some of the misunderstandings with friends is to educate them about diabetes and tell them ways that they can help you if you need it. This would be another time that you could look up T1D YouTube videos to share with them.

Tell your friends how you might act when your blood sugar is low or high and how they can help you. Make sure they know what a fast-acting snack is if you ever get a low around them. Let them know what they would have to do in an emergency situation for low blood sugar. Over time I've learned that friends can be great allies when it comes to diabetes, and most of your close friends will want to know more about it and how they can help you.

If you haven't already, what are some ways that you want to educate your friends about Type 1?

CHAPTER NINETEEN:
Peers with Diabetes

I believe that one of the most powerful resources a person with diabetes can have is friends and peers with diabetes. There is no one else in the world who truly knows how you feel except a fellow T1D. I know that I didn't find my confidence in diabetes until I found friends with diabetes. They inspired me to do better and be proud of my diabetes and the person it has made me. T1D friends are the only people you can truly laugh with about the funny things that happen to us. When you are down or experiencing a hard time with diabetes, they are the people who will support and inspire you to keep going. They are always there to share their experiences and knowledge to help you find more ways to help yourself. If you don't have any friends with diabetes yet, I strongly encourage you to reach out through events with the American Diabetes Association, JDRF, and Beyond Type 1, as well as safely online through Facebook pages or other diabetes communities.

Do you have friends with diabetes? If so, how have they helped you? How do you feel when you are around them?

_____

_____

_____

_____

_____

If you don't have friends with diabetes, how do you think you could benefit from meeting people with Type 1? How do you want to find peers with Type 1?

_____

_____

_____

_____

_____

_____

_____

_____

_____

_____

_____

_____

_____

Always remember to reach out to these friends when you are feeling down. They will always support you and make you feel less alone. I believe they are the most precious helpers you can have as a person living with Type 1.

Notes

CHAPTER TWENTY:

Independence

Readers of this book will be at different levels of independence depending on age, personality, and other factors. However, eventually all of us who live with Type 1 have to learn to manage diabetes on our own. One day you will move away from your parents/caregivers and will have to navigate many different aspects of being responsible for your diabetes. There is a lot of work and attention that goes into taking care of yourself when you live with a chronic condition. The day-to-day management may consist of monitoring blood sugar and administering insulin, but there are other responsibilities that come along when you are without your caregivers'/ family's help. You have to be responsible for buying healthy food, getting your insulin and diabetes supplies and making sure you don't run out of them, communicating with your doctor for continued care and refills, always making sure you have low treatment with you, keeping track of when you have to change your pump sites or CGM, and educating the people around you about diabetes so that you are safe—and more. It can be overwhelming at times and may be scary at first.

How do you feel about becoming more independent with your diabetes management?

What frustrations or worries have you experienced with becoming more independent?

what do you see for your future away from your parents/ caregivers?

_____

_____

_____

_____

_____

_____

_____

_____

_____

_____

_____

_____

It can be really exciting to move away from your family and become more independent. However, you have to make sure that you're ready for the responsibility of managing your diabetes on your own. Prepare yourself by making sure you know how to do some of the things I listed above. Speak to your parents/caregivers about how they can continue to support you and teach you about becoming more independent. If you move out and live with roommates, make sure you educate them about diabetes and tell them ways that they can help you. Make sure they know how to help you in case of an emergency. Always have a plan for your safety. If you ever live alone, make sure you have a plan for if you need help; have someone who lives close by that could help you if you ever needed it.

What are some plans you have for living independently with diabetes?

_____

_____

_____

_____

_____

_____

_____

_____

_____

_____

_____

_____

_____

_____

_____

_____

_____

Notes

CHAPTER TWENTY-ONE

Creating Identity and Making Meaning

As a teen, you are figuring out who you are. You're trying to find what speaks to you and create an identity. Sometimes it can feel like diabetes is a huge part of your life and therefore a huge part of your identity. The chronic nature of diabetes makes it bleed into every aspect of your life. It affects your physical, mental, social, and spiritual lives. But while you are a person who has Type 1 diabetes, diabetes alone does not define you. You are so much more than a person who lives with diabetes.

Still, I believe it's extremely important to find meaning and create a part of our identity from our experience of living with Type 1 diabetes. We all learn from our life experiences, and we can take what we learn and create meaning from those experiences. When we create meaning from something, it gives us a larger sense of the world and ourselves. Sometimes it can also show us a purpose to our struggle. To create meaning from diabetes is not to be thankful for it but to recognize what it has added to your lives. I don't expect that all of you will be at the point where you can fully accept diabetes as a part of your identity or recognize the meaning that it has added to your life. It's OK if you are not at this point; I hope that one day you will be.

How is diabetes a part of your identity?

_____

_____

_____

_____

_____

_____

_____

_____

_____

_____

_____

_____

_____

_____

_____

_____

It may be hard to think of good things about living with Type 1, but there is probably something positive that has made you proud of yourself for living through and surviving with diabetes.

what makes you proud about living with Type 1 diabetes?

What have you learned from living with diabetes?

_____

_____

_____

_____

_____

_____

_____

_____

_____

_____

_____

_____

_____

_____

_____

_____

_____

_____

Many people can create meaning from what they have learned from diabetes. If you don't feel this way, that's OK.

what meaning has been added to your life because you live with diabetes?

_____

_____

_____

_____

_____

_____

_____

_____

_____

_____

_____

_____

_____

_____

_____

_____

_____

_____

_____

_____

_____

_____

How do these things make you feel?

_____

_____

_____

_____

_____

_____

_____

_____

_____

_____

_____

_____

_____

_____

I have learned so many things from living with diabetes. I wouldn't be the person I am today without diabetes. I believe by finding meaning and creating a part of our identity from living with diabetes, we can live more fully and more lovingly toward our bodies and our experiences with diabetes.

In Closing

Thank you for reading and using this journal. I sincerely hope that you have been able to learn from this journal and express some emotions through it. My mission for creating this journal was to have a space where teens could express themselves and learn more about Type 1 and their experiences. I hope that you have learned how to have self-compassion and understanding. I hope you know that you are never alone. There is always support to be found in the Type 1 community. I hope that you can keep this journal as a reminder to allow for intense emotions to be felt and expressed and to remember your experiences and grow from them.

Living with Type 1 is a challenge. The emotions you experience along the way are valid and are meant to be felt. You are valuable. Living with Type 1 shows your strength and resilience. I hope you can accept the meaning and lessons that come with living with Type 1. Allow it to show you how special you are and how much growth and strength you have.

In writing this book, I've learned even more about T1D and my experience with it. I still have a lot more to learn from the readers of this book and hope that one day I can meet you and hear your story.

Please take care of yourself and be kind to yourself.

Living with Type 1 Diabetes

I have the right to feel how I feel about my diabetes.

I have the right to express my feelings about my diabetes.

I have the right to get upset about my diabetes when I'm having a hard time.

I have the right to talk and ask questions about my diabetes.

I have the right to need other people to help me with my diabetes, especially my caregivers, friends, doctors, nurses, teachers, coaches, and other adults.

I have the right to teach others about my diabetes when they don't understand.

I have the right to question why I have diabetes and others don't.

I have the right to do all kinds of activities regardless of my diabetes, as long as I am safe and feel good.

I have the right to express myself when I don't feel good.

I have the right to advocate for my body and health so I can live my best life.